Phoenician ship

Viking long boat

Galleon

Galley ship

Treasure Thieves

on the High Seas: Pirates, Privateers, and Plunder

Roxie Munro

HOLIDAY HOUSE  NEW YORK

To my sailing siblings–Ann Munro Wood, Robert Aaron Munro, and Suzanne Munro Gubbings. May you have fair winds, following seas, and blue skies forever.

Printed and bound in October 2025 at C&C Offset, Shenzhen, China.
The artwork was created with India ink and colored acrylic inks on 100% rag paper.
www.holidayhouse.com
First Edition
1 3 5 7 9 10 8 6 4 2

Library of Congress Cataloging-in-Publication Data is available.

ISBN: 978-0-8234-5947-6 (hardcover)

EU Authorized Representative: HackettFlynn Ltd, 36 Cloch Choirneal, Balrothery, Co. Dublin, K32 C942, Ireland. EU@walkerpublishinggroup.com

Table of Contents

The Pirate Queen of Ireland

When she was a young girl of eleven or twelve, Grace O'Malley was told she could not travel on a sea expedition with her father. They said her long hair would be caught in the ropes. So the feisty Grace, embarrassing and amusing her family, cut off all her hair. It earned her the nickname "Gráinne Mhaol," which means "Bald Grace" in Irish.

Grace was fascinated by the sea and refused to obey her family's orders to stay closer to home and the land.

Grace O'Malley was born in 1530 into a great seafaring clan that had controlled lands on the West Coast of Ireland for three hundred years. Unlike most of the Irish chieftains who made their living by farming, her family fished, traded, and taxed others. They built castle strongholds in strategic positions along the coast, much of which they dominated.

Grace was an adventurous noblewoman who spent much of her life at sea. Although a lot of her youth and young adulthood was spent on a ship, she received formal education and learned to speak foreign languages. Her father respected her intelligence, courage, and strength, and after his death she inherited her father's position instead of his oldest son.

She married twice, securing more wealth and power both times. Grace O'Malley had three children by her first husband, the heir to a neighboring clan. He introduced her to pirating. When he was murdered by a nearby clan, she defeated them and kept his castle. She married her second husband to increase her land holdings and naval fleet. She divorced him after a year but kept his castle too. Rumor has it that Grace gave birth to their son at sea and was nursing the infant below decks a few hours after he was born when they were attacked by North African pirates. She wrapped the baby in a blanket, charged up on deck, fired a musket, rallied her crew, and helped capture the enemy. At one point, she commanded three galleys and twenty ships, and captained two hundred men.

During Grace O'Malley's lifetime, the English were taking control of Ireland. They labeled Grace a pirate for harassing their ships, and she spent time in jail. But when the English governor of her region captured two of her sons and her half-brother, she sailed to London and negotiated their release with Queen Elizabeth I, promising to stop supporting Irish lords who wanted independence. Both women met some, but not all, of the demands they'd agreed upon. Later Grace returned to supporting Irish insurgents.

Her biographer Anne Chambers called Grace an accomplished mariner, a ruthless plunderer, a mercenary, and a woman who refused to allow any barrier to obstruct her, saying, "She commanded loyalty because she was braver than the men."

The Dragon

Captain Francis Drake hatched a plan. His ship, the *Golden Hind*, was sailing north up the west coast of South America, quietly chasing the *Cacafuego*, a Spanish ship loaded with gold, precious gems, and lots of silver. At that time, Peruvian mines produced more silver than all the other countries in the world combined. But the weight of all that silver made the *Cacafuego* cumbersome to handle, and it wallowed in the water. The *Golden Hind* was speedy—too speedy.

To sneak up on the *Cacafuego* while pretending to be a friendly boat, Drake tied weighted wine barrels to the hull and threw them overboard to slow his boat down without lowering any sails. The Spanish ship wasn't suspicious and didn't prepare for battle. The *Golden Hind* came alongside, and Drake's men jumped aboard. The *Cacafuego* crew surrendered fast. Drake treated them well—he dined with the officers and important passengers, dropped them off safely at a nearby port, and even gave some of them presents.

Drake had left England a year earlier, in 1577. He crossed the Atlantic, headed down along the east coast of South America, and navigated through the dangerous Strait of Magellan. Two ships in his convoy sank in violent weather and seven had to return to England. His ship, the *Golden Hind*, was the only one to make it through.

After loading up on the *Cacafuego*'s treasures (it took six days to transfer the loot to Drake's ship), he continued north along the Pacific Coast and headed across the Pacific Ocean to return to England the long way around. He arrived back in Plymouth more than two years later, the first Englishman to circumnavigate the globe.

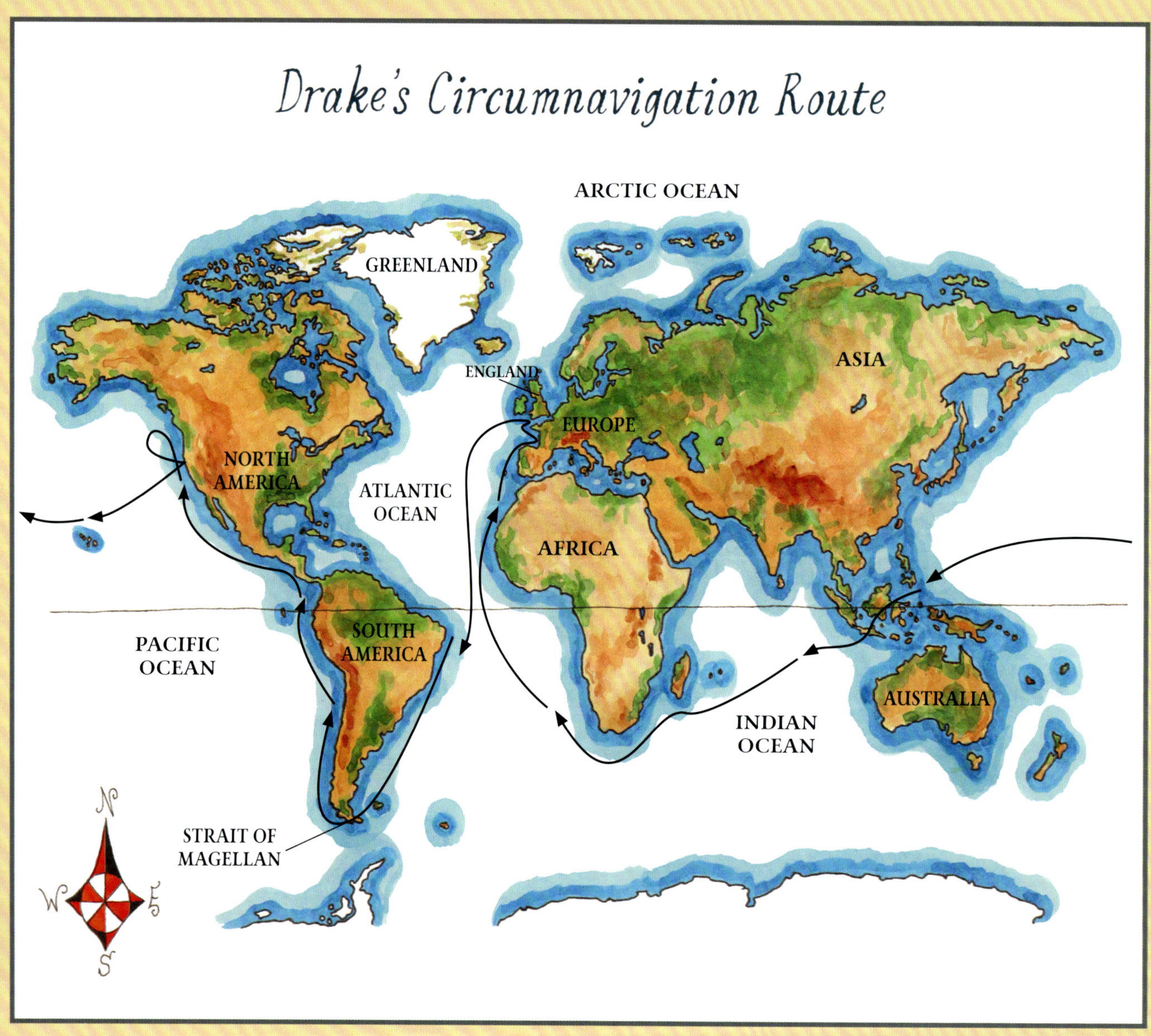

The Spanish ship's treasure included thirteen chests full of jewels, eighty pounds of gold, and at least twenty-five tons of silver.

Like many of that time, Drake switched between being a privateer and a pirate. Queen Elizabeth I had given him license to be a privateer, but she secretly sanctioned piracy. Her share of the plunder from the *Cacafuego* was greater than her entire revenue that year from taxes and crown lands combined. Drake transported twenty tons of silver, gold, and jewels to the Tower of London for the Queen. She publicly called him "My Pirate" and made him a knight: Sir Francis Drake.

Drake, the second-highest earning pirate of all time, had come from a humble background in Devonshire, England. The boy started his career at sea when he was thirteen years old and then became a superstar. The public avidly read the illustrated news sheets and stories about his adventures in a series of pamphlets. The Spanish called him "El Dragon," "The Dragon" in English. In 1587 alone, he burned more than twenty vessels in just one port.

In 1588, the King of Spain sent the massive Spanish Armada, which included 150 ships and eighteen thousand men, to attack England. Sir Francis Drake, the second-in-command of the English fleet, helped defeat the invaders and received national renown.

Afterward, he returned with more than two dozen ships to the Spanish Main across the Atlantic, but in 1596 he caught a fever, became deathly ill, and was buried at sea off the coast of Panama.

Sir Francis Drake died a national hero and is still remembered as one of England's greatest sea captains.

The Biggest Prize Ever

It was the largest treasure haul ever captured by pirates. The big ship, named *Ganj-i-Sawai*, was owned by the Grand Moghul of India and had sixty-two guns and four or five hundred guards carrying small arms. There were six hundred other passengers.

When the pirate Henry Avery and his crew of 113 men jumped aboard the *Ganj-i-Sawai*, a violent fight followed. Eventually the pirates overpowered the vessel and its crew, passengers, and slaves. Avery's men brutally tortured the crew until they told them where the treasures were. The pirates were stunned to realize that, of the twenty-five vessels traveling in the Indian fleet, twenty-three of which got away, this one was by far the most valuable. The conquest made them the richest pirates in history.

Not much is known about Henry Avery's early life, partly because he used many different names, or aliases, during his lifetime. Henry Every, John Avery, Long Ben, and Benjamin Bridgeman were a few. He was probably born in Plymouth, England. His first jobs at sea were on merchant vessels, some of which were slave traders.

Early in 1694, Avery became a first mate on a Spanish privateer ship called *Charles II* chasing after French smugglers in the Caribbean. But the mostly English crew was ill-treated by the drunken captain. They talked Avery into leading a mutiny and took over the large, speedy, forty-six-gun ship, renaming it the *Fancy*, and became pirates, attacking Dutch and English merchant vessels off the coast of Africa. They made their base on the island of Madagascar, a haven convenient for attacking the richly laden vessels in the Indian Ocean traveling between India and Arabia and on to Europe.

By 1695, Avery commanded a group of six pirate ships. He modified his own ship, the *Fancy*, to make it one of the faster ships actively prowling the Indian Ocean.

When Avery's pirates captured the *Ganj-i-Sawai*, the treasure included gold; silver; jewels like diamonds, emeralds, and rubies; and a magnificent gold saddle and bridle encrusted with incredibly valuable gems including rubies, worth much more than the haul from the other Indian ship they had also conquered. Each pirate received one thousand English pounds. It would take an honest seaman eighty years to earn that much! And Captain Avery, and his officers, got much more. Avery had promised to share the booty with the five other pirate ships in the group, but in the night, his ship sneaked away with all the treasure.

No one knows exactly what happened to Avery. After this super successful haul, he was never heard from again.

The Most Successful Buccaneer

How did a herd of cows help this motley group of ruthless buccaneers, ex-soldiers, runaway slaves, European immigrants, and sailors conquer the second-biggest city in the Western Hemisphere?

It was the largest battle fought in the Americas before the eighteenth century and went on for days: the sack of the port of Panama, the major prize of the Spanish Main. In 1671, it was destroyed and burned to the ground by Henry Morgan and his pirates.

In 1670, Morgan set out with thirty-three ships and two thousand buccaneers to attack Panama City. After landing on the eastern Caribbean coast, they spent days working their way westward through the jungle to the city on the Pacific coast.

At one point they were so hungry, they ate tree bark, leaves, and even their leather bags.

When they arrived at their goal, they were exhausted and needed food. Morgan's crew was outnumbered but helped out by a failed Spanish trick. The Spaniards had brought herds of cattle to the battle outside the city to confuse the invading pirates. But, frightened by the gunfire, the cattle turned around and stampeded back through the Spanish troops, causing chaos, injuries, and finally, defeat.

Although Morgan and his men prevailed, there wasn't much loot. In advance, the port authorities had sent most treasure to Ecuador. The disappointed buccaneers spent the next month destroying what was left of the city, burning and looting, and torturing their prisoners.

It turned out to be Henry Morgan's last great raid.

For years Morgan had used Port Royal, Jamaica, as his base. He went back and forth between piracy (when he and his crew got all the loot) and privateering (when he had to share the plunder with the government).

Morgan raided from Cuba to Venezuela, from Hispaniola to Panama, terrorizing the Spanish Main. He attacked with discipline, savagery, and brutality. When his eight hundred men once won a town on the island of Cuba, they threatened to chop the wives and children of the townspeople to pieces if they didn't surrender. People were imprisoned in the village churches by the merciless buccaneers and died of starvation.

Morgan was sent back to England, but despite his cruel deeds and legal troubles, he had friends there, as well as wealth. He was let go. He was knighted by the king and returned to his lands and his family in Jamaica.

Sir Henry Morgan accumulated quite a lot of riches from his pirating activities. He became the lieutenant governor of Jamaica, retired from pirating, and lived on a big plantation.

One of his major claims to fame is still evident today—there is a famous brand of spiced rum made only in Jamaica called "Captain Morgan." You can see him on the label in full pirate regalia with cutlass, keg, and tricorn pirate hat.

25th/1699
Capt William Kid
Earl of Bellmont
357
Gold
49½ grams
203.
4⅓ grams

The Unluckiest Pirate

Jonathan Gardiner, a farmer on a small island near the tip of eastern Long Island in New York, wrote up a list of Captain Kidd's treasure late in the seventeenth century. Legend has it that Kidd asked the farmer to hide the valuables for him. They included bags of gold and silver dust, coins, and bars; jewels and precious stones; bags of sugar; candlesticks; decorative jars; canvas; and more. He hoped they would be picked up by his friend, Englishman Richard Coote, the British governor of New York and Massachusetts at the time. Kidd thought the governor would help him with his political troubles back in England.

William Kidd, born in Scotland in 1645, went to work on the high seas after his seaman father died and left the family poor. He became a successful Caribbean privateer for the English. In New York, he married a wealthy, twice-widowed woman; had two daughters; and was considered an honest, hardworking captain who sometimes accepted privateering assignments.

He returned to England to combat piracy, particularly by England's enemy France. As with most privateers, the government signed a contract allowing Kidd to attack pirates. He sailed to New York to sign on a carefully picked crew of about 150 experienced privateers. But the British Royal Navy appropriated more than half his professional crew and replaced them with convicted criminals and hardened pirates.

They went east to the Indian Ocean where his crew pressured him to turn into a pirate. At one point, Kidd struck the ship's gunner on the head with a bucket, unintentionally killing him.

He captured a French merchant ship with an English captain. Kidd tried to give up the prize when he learned about the captain, but his crew refused. Kidd was labeled a pirate. Still looking for real pirate ships, Kidd found one off the east coast of Africa, but instead of capturing it, most of his crew joined it.

Kidd and his thirteen remaining loyal crew members sailed to Boston, where Kidd tried to get a pardon from his friend, Governor Richard Coote. But Coote had Kidd arrested and sent to England, where Kidd was imprisoned and went on trial for the death of the gunner and multiple counts of piracy.

There was misinformation about Kidd in the London newspapers blaming him for atrocities his nasty crew committed. Papers proving his innocence were "lost" (but turned up hundreds of years later).

He was found guilty and hanged at the famous "Execution Dock." His body was put into a vertical open cage with iron bars, where, for three years, it stayed up on the banks of the River Thames as a warning to other pirates.

But there is still a mystery . . . the treasure he gave to Gardiner was probably recovered by his "friend" Governor Richard Coote, but no one is sure Coote got it all. People are still hunting for Captain Kidd's treasure.

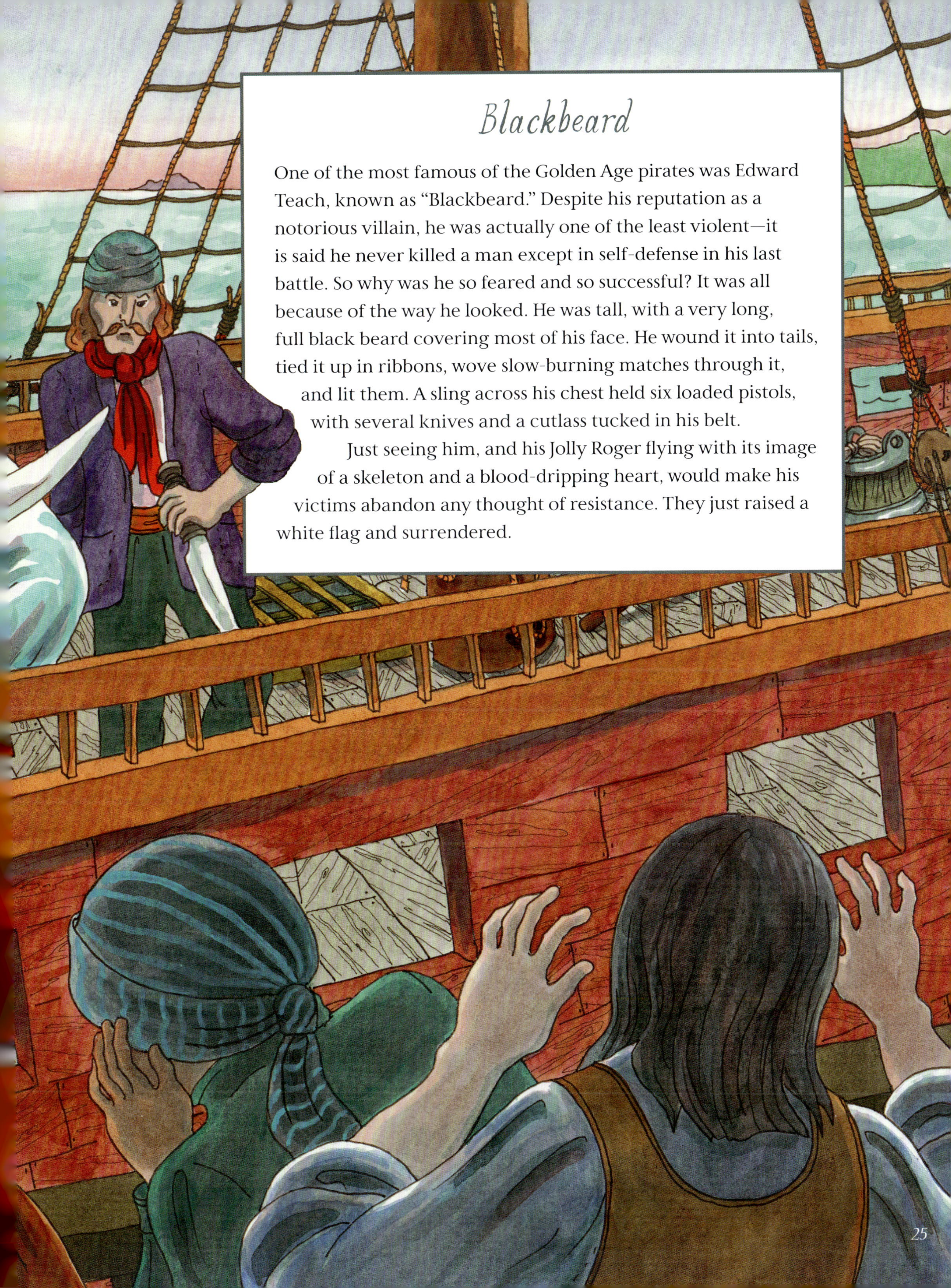

Blackbeard

One of the most famous of the Golden Age pirates was Edward Teach, known as "Blackbeard." Despite his reputation as a notorious villain, he was actually one of the least violent—it is said he never killed a man except in self-defense in his last battle. So why was he so feared and so successful? It was all because of the way he looked. He was tall, with a very long, full black beard covering most of his face. He wound it into tails, tied it up in ribbons, wove slow-burning matches through it, and lit them. A sling across his chest held six loaded pistols, with several knives and a cutlass tucked in his belt.

Just seeing him, and his Jolly Roger flying with its image of a skeleton and a blood-dripping heart, would make his victims abandon any thought of resistance. They just raised a white flag and surrendered.

As a teenager in the early 1700s, Edward Teach left England for the Caribbean. He worked on a privateer's vessel and then on a pirate ship. Intelligent, generous, and well-educated, he soon had his own command and began capturing other ships including a big three-hundred-ton frigate which he renamed *Queen Anne's Revenge*.

In 1718, from a base on Ocracoke Island off North Carolina, he began robbing passing ships and soon commanded four vessels and more than three hundred pirates. He bribed the governor to avoid arrest. At one point, Blackbeard laid siege to Charles Town in South Carolina and seized eight ships.

The governor of Virginia got increasingly irritated with Blackbeard's exploits and hired two naval vessels, named *Jane* and *Ranger*, with a total of fifty-eight soldiers as a pirate-hunting force. When the troops arrived in an inlet off Ocracoke, Blackbeard had spent the week before partying to celebrate a recent raid, and at least twenty of his crew were on shore taking a break.

Although the pirate ship's big cannons did a lot of damage to the smaller naval ships, the captain of one of the larger naval vessels, *Jane*, had a plan to outsmart the pirates. Captain Maynard had his soldiers hide below decks, so when Blackbeard's crew boarded the boat, they saw only the captain and one crew member. Suddenly soldiers burst up from the cabin below with pistols, swords, daggers, cutlasses, and axes. Blackbeard was killed by a Scotsman. His head was cut off and hung on the bowsprit of the *Jane*.

Although Blackbeard was only a pirate captain for two years, he is legendary.

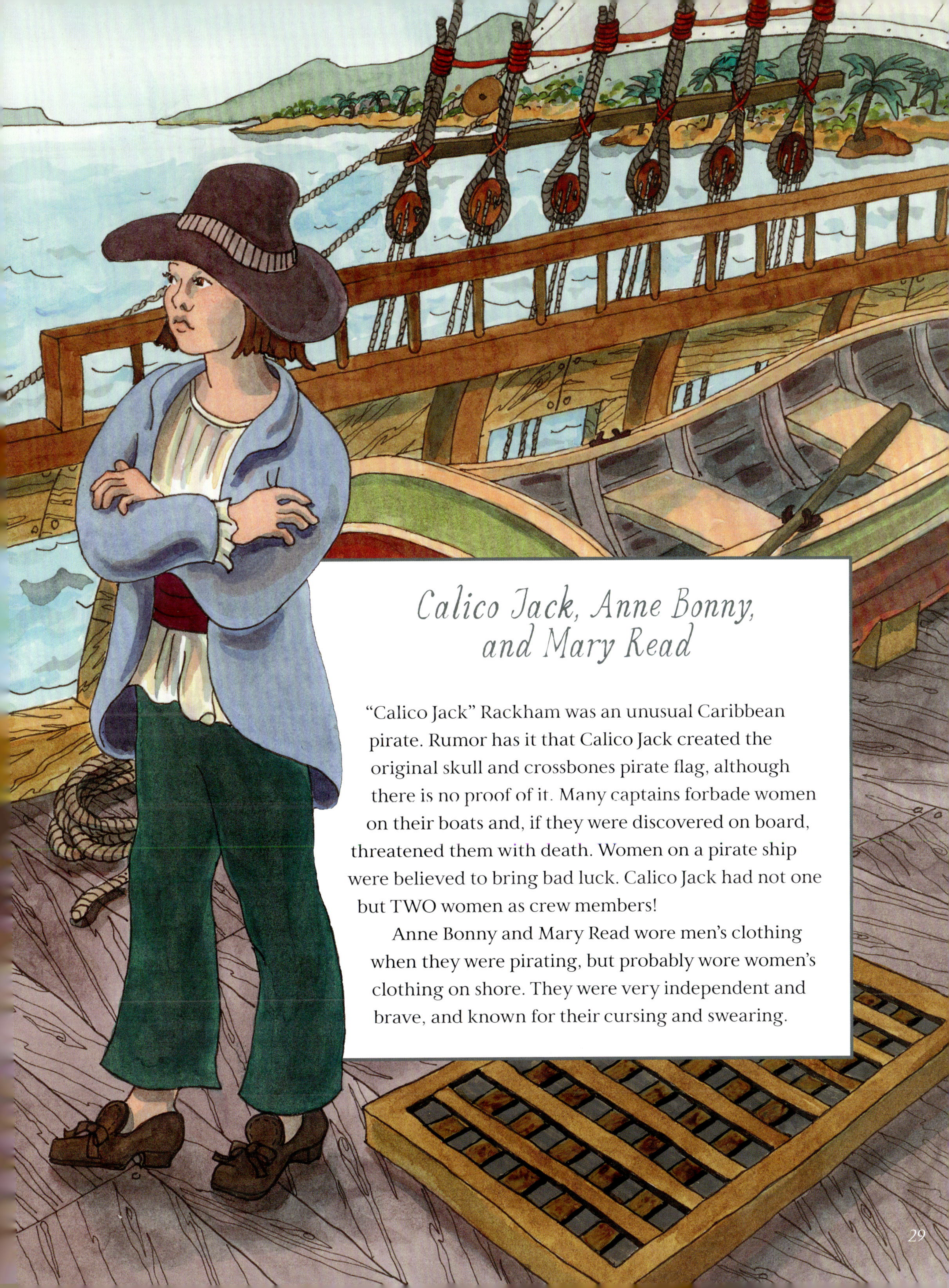

Calico Jack, Anne Bonny, and Mary Read

"Calico Jack" Rackham was an unusual Caribbean pirate. Rumor has it that Calico Jack created the original skull and crossbones pirate flag, although there is no proof of it. Many captains forbade women on their boats and, if they were discovered on board, threatened them with death. Women on a pirate ship were believed to bring bad luck. Calico Jack had not one but TWO women as crew members!

Anne Bonny and Mary Read wore men's clothing when they were pirating, but probably wore women's clothing on shore. They were very independent and brave, and known for their cursing and swearing.

Anne Bonny was probably from County Cork, Ireland, the child of a disgraced married lawyer named Cormac and a family servant. Cormac; his daughter, Anne; and her mom moved to a plantation in South Carolina.

Anne was a feisty, sometimes violent girl. She married a small-time pirate named James Bonny when she was a teenager and went to the Caribbean with him, where she met Calico Jack Rackham. They fell in love. Calico Jack offered James money to divorce her, but he refused, so Calico Jack and Anne ran away together to continue pirating.

Mary Read was born in England. It's said she had a harsh childhood. Legend has it that she was raised as a boy as a ruse to make her grandmother think she was her favored, deceased half-brother and continue to support her and her mom. Even after her grandmother died when she was thirteen, Mary still pretended to be a boy. She worked as a manservant and joined the Royal Navy and then the army. She served as a soldier in the Netherlands and even got promoted. Later she boarded a Dutch ship with English soldiers going to the Caribbean.

They were attacked by Calico Jack Rackman. He made the English soldiers on the ship become his crew. Mary liked the idea of being a pirate and stayed on. She and Anne Bonny soon became friends.

Calico Jack was named "Calico" (which means "multicolored") because he liked to wear fine printed cotton clothing.

The captain and his crew were eventually hunted down by the authorities off the island of Jamaica. The pirate crew was partying and drinking, and most were too drunk to fight. They hid below decks, including Calico Jack. According to legend, Anne Bonny and Mary Read alone fought valiantly against the pirate hunters. Calico Jack gave up without much of a fight. He went on trial in Jamaica and was hanged at Gallows Point. His career as a pirate had lasted less than three years. Anne said that she was sorry to see him executed but commented, "If you had fought like a man, you need not have been hang'd like a dog."

The two women were also jailed but were spared, the only women known to be convicted of piracy. Mary died of a fever in prison but Anne Bonny probably lived on. Little is known of her, though some reports say she eventually got out of jail and went on to live a long, quiet life.

The Gentle Pirate

Captain Edward England was a kind and merciful pirate. He let many of his victims go free, sometimes even gave them ships, and was hesitant to torture or kill captured crews and captains. In the end, his empathy destroyed him. Many of his officers and crew were more bloodthirsty, and they eventually turned on him.

John Taylor, a once-trusted shipmate to whom Captain England had earlier given a ship to command, organized a rebellion among the crew. Most of them joined the mutiny and removed the compassionate England from his position as captain. They set Captain England and three of his loyal crew members ashore on a small island called Mauritius in the middle of the Indian Ocean, seven hundred miles east of Madagascar, off the coast of Africa, with a keg of water and no food. Marooned!

Edward England was born in Ireland in the late seventeenth century. A skilled sailor and an educated man, he worked as a regular seaman in the Caribbean and off the coast of Florida. When his ship was captured by the pirate Christopher Winter, he had to join the crew. After working with another famous pirate, Charles Vane, as a quartermaster (second-in-command), he got his own ship.

When the governor of the Bahamas, Woodes Rogers, started vigorously going after pirates, England set out for Africa in a stolen sloop with a new crew.

When his crew started murdering and torturing captive sailors, England made them stop. He was known as "the Merciful." He spared many men whom others would have killed. England pretended to be a legitimate privateer for a while, tricking West African officials in the Portuguese, English, and Dutch African areas and raiding their forts.

England infuriated John Taylor, now the captain of one of England's ships, by allowing a cargo captain and crew to live after the other captain had killed many of England's crew. Taylor rallied most of Captain England's crew to mutiny, taking over his ship and marooning him.

England and the three crew members had been put ashore on the isolated island of Mauritius with only some water and a pistol and gunpowder to shoot themselves if all looked bleak. But England managed to find food and, after four months, they had built a small boat or raft. They sailed the seven hundred miles to Madagascar, an island off the East African coast. It was conveniently located to use as a pirate base to attack trading ships traveling the Indian Ocean on the way to Europe and was a safe haven, friendly to pirates.

Other pirates helped him out for a while. It was said that he became a beggar, starving in the slums of Madagascar. Sadly, one of the most humane pirate captains ever ended up soon dying, probably of a tropical illness, as a poor, sick man.

The Indian Ocean

Black Bart

Nicknamed "Black Bart" because of his black hair and dark skin, Welshman Bartholomew Roberts loved to dress grandly, even in battle. He often wore a crimson waistcoat, an expensive hat with bright feathers, scarlet pants, and, around his neck, a heavy gold chain with a diamond cross. Black Bart was believed to be one of the most successful pirates ever—he plundered more than four hundred vessels in two and a half years, terrorizing ships in the waters of the Caribbean, off the east coast of South America, along the American colonies, and along Newfoundland and West Africa.

Early on in his pirate career, he captured a large French ship and took it for his own. He renamed it *Royal Fortune*. After that, almost every time he got a new vessel for his fleet, he used "Fortune" in the name. There were at least four *Royal Fortunes*.

Black Bart was born John Roberts in South Wales. He worked on a Caribbean slave ship, which was captured by a famous pirate named Howell Davis. Black Bart found he liked being a pirate. He became known for his excellent navigational skills. When Davis was killed in an ambush, Black Bart was elected the new captain.

It was said that, unlike most pirates, Black Bart did not drink alcohol or swear, and he observed the Sabbath. He was said to have refused to attack other ships on a Sunday. But he was known to be vicious, and brutally murdered many opposing crew members and slaves. Sometimes just raising Black Bart's black flag put so much fear into trading ships' captains that they gave up without firing a shot.

Many pirates wrote "Articles of Agreement," or codes of conduct, for their crews to sign. Black Bart's was one of the most extensive, with eleven detailed regulations. They included giving each man an equal vote in the ship's affairs, as well as specific shares of liquor. Precise

equations were followed for dividing up the loot. There were severe punishments, like having your nose and ears slit or being marooned on an island, for robbing another crew member, stealing from the plunder, or gambling. Lights and candles had to be out by 8:00 p.m. according to the rules. They had to keep guns and cutlasses clean and ready for action. Death to anyone for letting a boy or a woman stay on board. Death to anyone deserting during a battle. And the ship's musicians were allowed to rest on Sundays but were required to play the other six days.

Early in his career, Black Bart said that his motto was "a merry life and a short one." And he did die young, in his late thirties. In his brief time as a pirate, in addition to being known as one of the most violent, he was also recognized as the best dressed pirate ever.

When the British Royal Navy killed Black Bart in 1722, it was considered the end of the Golden Age of Piracy.

The Chinese Woman Pirate, Boss of Eighty Thousand Men

They swarmed over the flotilla like bees. It was a classic "shock and awe" military tactic. Hundreds of fast Chinese junks, part of a four-hundred-ship pirate fleet, pounced on the group of European trading ships in an overwhelming onslaught in the South China Sea.

The leader of this group of pirate junks, called the Red Flag Fleet, was a formidable woman named Ching Shih. She had ordered the raids. The Red Flag Fleet was part of a larger pirate group of six fleets known by the color of their flags—red (the biggest group), black, blue, white, yellow, and purple. Ching, the commander of the whole pirate confederation, was said to have controlled at least 1,800 junks and up to eighty thousand men.

Ching Shih is known by several names, including Cheng I Sao, Shih Yang, and Zheng Yi Sao. She was born into a poor family who lived and worked on board junks along the China coast. When she was older, she worked in a floating gambling house.

In 1801, at the age of twenty-six, she married the commander of the powerful Red Flag Fleet of pirate ships. It's thought he married her because of her reputation as a shrewd businesswoman. She demanded equal control of his pirate fleet as soon as they married, and when he died six years later, she became the commander of the whole six-fleet pirate confederation.

Like many pirate bosses, she and her second, younger husband had a detailed list of rules for her pirates. Offenders could be beheaded for disobeying orders, harming women captives, not distributing loot fairly a second time (the first time, they were just beaten), or deserting their post a second time (the first time, just their ears were cut off). Treasure was counted, registered, and distributed to the crew according to careful calculations.

Unlike on Western pirate ships, in China, women were allowed on board pirate junks. They often worked alongside men, sometimes even commanding the junk.

The pirate confederation was well organized. They pounced on smaller junks close to shore for food and equipment, and preyed on larger, oceangoing vessels for valuable cargo. They took villagers captive for ransom and raided government properties for weapons. They operated through terror and were often violent and savage.

For a decade, Ching Shih controlled the giant pirate fleet, seizing many ships, kidnapping foreign officials for ransom, and destroying numerous villages and towns. After battling the pirates for years, the Chinese government agreed to negotiate with Ching, who was also tired of the pressure and harassment. The government was desperate to end the piracy. In exchange for giving up thousands of pirates, hundreds of ships, and many weapons, Ching got to keep some ships. Her pirates could either join the government military force fighting other pirates or return to their rural countryside. In addition, she got a pardon, a cash settlement, and a title. Ching went back into business as a successful gambling house owner. She was widely respected and lived to be almost seventy.

The Pirate Life

There have been pirates around since humans started using boats. They were active in ancient times and still are. The adventures here cover pirates who operated in oceans and seas all over the world. Until a few hundred years ago, there weren't reliable records, but the individual stories in this book come from written accounts.

Early "Sea People" from 1200 BCE and earlier raided towns and cities along the Mediterranean coast in boats with oars and sometimes a simple sail. The Phoenician and Greek pirates also operated in the Mediterranean Sea. They preferred shallow-bottomed boats which were fast and easy to maneuver and could sail where larger vessels could not, such as over rocks near the shores. The ships they attacked used coastal routes rather than the open ocean, so it was easy for pirates to hide in the many islands and inlets.

During the Middle Ages, all sorts of vandals raided ships and coastal villages. From the late eighth century to the early twelfth, Norse Vikings made vicious pirates. The northern raiders' wild appearances were terrifying. Norwegians traveled west to pillage and plunder the British Isles and beyond, including Iceland and Greenland. Swedish and Danish Vikings went east—down the European rivers and into Russia via the Baltic Sea. They used the sun and stars to navigate. Viking ships were built for speed, agility, and stability with keels (a long piece of wood along the bottom of the boat) that were shallow and extra strong so they could travel not only in coastal waters but also in the open sea. They could put up a big rectangular sail but used oars, manned by slaves, in shallow waters and rivers.

The Golden Age of Piracy began after Europeans discovered North and South America, which they called the New World. Its riches—gold, silver, gemstones, sugar, and more—attracted all sorts of people. An area mostly claimed by Spain, known as the Spanish Main, included parts of Mexico, Central America, South America, and many Caribbean islands. Portugal, France, and England also fought over the lands and resources found there.

During the Golden Age of Piracy, which lasted from approximately 1650 to 1730 CE, there were several types of pirates. Most were basic violent robbers. Some were privateers. Those were legal pirates, sanctioned and carrying an official government-written agreement called a "Letter of Marque" allowing them to raid and attack an enemy country's vessels. The privateers' plunder was shared with the country with which they signed the license. Then, there were buccaneers. The name comes from Caribbean hunters who cured meat in boucans, a kind of grill. They were a lawless group and banded together when the Spanish tried to drive them out of Hispaniola (now Haiti and the Dominican Republic). Many were cruel cutthroats who preyed upon Spanish ships. They are said to have invented the cutlass, creating it by shortening a long sword used to butcher meat.

Beginning in the sixteenth century, Islamic corsairs, often called Barbary pirates, were based on the coast of North Africa and pounced on trade ships in the Mediterranean and beyond, including coastal areas of Ireland and the British Isles. As did most invaders, they often kept captured crewmen as slaves to work or to sell. They had big sailing galleys with rowers. As many as six slaves were required to pull each of the huge oars on those ships.

There was also pirating along the east coast of Africa, in the Indian Ocean, where the rich European-Indian trade route sprang up. The Far East was also a hotbed of pirating. Eventually, authorities all over the world cracked down on pirates, capturing and executing many of them.

People became pirates because they were captured crew, released or escaped slaves, or former soldiers, or sometimes by ambition or choice. They were of many different races, and most were illiterate. Life was often short and brutal.

What was it like to live on a pirate ship? Crowded. Many people were needed to fight, as well as to work as crew. There were no showers or bathtubs. People were dirty and smelly, and rarely washed or changed their clothes. Most pirates stole their clothes from people they captured. On the ship, they usually went barefoot. Boots were too clumsy. They slept where they could, curled up on the top deck, lying among the barrels and equipment below decks, or in hammocks slung up between wooden beams. The toilet was a wooden plank with a hole in it placed up near the bowsprit over the water at the front of the ship. There were lice, fleas, cockroaches, and rats. It was stinky on board since people shared their space with live chickens, pigs, and even cows, which would eventually be had for dinner. It was hard to keep enough fresh water to drink, so they often mixed it with rum or beer.

Pirates often got scurvy, a painful disease caused by lack of vitamin C. Their teeth would rot and need to be pulled out by pliers. Their skin would blacken and develop sores. It even affected their limbs and brains.

The lowest deck of the ship had to be pumped out frequently. Foul-smelling stagnant water sloshed around the bottom, or bilge, of the ship. But the captain and senior officers often had their own quarters, usually high up in the stern, or rear, of the boat, where it was cleaner than below decks and safer from attacks.

What are some of the myths about pirates? Many are not true, invented to make novels more exciting and movies and plays more dramatic. There's only one recorded instance, and it may not be true, of a Danish pirate captain making prisoners "walk the plank." Little is documented about having a parrot as a pet, although pirate cargo was sometimes exotic animals, so perhaps a captain or crew member kept a parrot once in a while for amusement. High boots above the knee are also a product of movie fiction. In real life, they are too hard to maneuver in while fighting. Some pirates did wear gold earrings. It was a way of showing (and saving) their share of the treasure. And it is true that eyepatches, peg legs, and hooks for missing hands or arms were used.

Many pirate captains made their crew sign a set of rules when they arrived on board. They were surprisingly democratic; for example, captains were crew members who were elected or chosen by the crew. And they could be "fired." An abusive or disliked captain could be voted off the boat, or be left marooned on a desert island, or return to being just another crew member.

Although there were strict rules about distributing the booty to the crew and officers (and sometimes government officials), many pirates lost most of their share when they finally went ashore after a session of pirating and plundering. They'd drink, smoke, and spend it on partying, and often went back to sea broke. But they generally made much more than a regular soldier or merchant seaman.

When "guns" on a vessel are referred to, such as a "twenty-four-gun galleon," it means available cannons. They were often used to hit a ship broadside (firing cannonballs into one side of the hull). Other weapons were handheld cutlasses, knives, and flintlock revolvers. Fighting equipment included a grappling iron, a tool like an anchor with barbed points to securely hold the rigging of another ship close by a rope attached to the top of it, so pirates could board. One of the tricks defending sailors used was to grease the deck or scatter dried peas so invaders would slip and fall when they boarded. Pirates also threw small metal spikes on the deck so barefoot sailors would cut their feet. They sometimes made a smokescreen of burning smelly sulfur to confuse fighters, or they'd throw primitive versions of a Molotov cocktail, homemade grenades in a jar or a bottle with a smoldering mix of flammable tar and rags.

We still have pirates. They are operating right now in the Caribbean, usually stealing or robbing small, private sailing craft. There are modern-day pirates in the Gulf of Aden, off the Arabian Peninsula and the east coast of Africa, pouncing on everything from sailboats to giant container ships. In East Asia, pirates attack fishing boats and cargo ships as well as private vessels. Like earlier pirates, they often kidnap people for ransom and forced labor.

Pirates have been plundering and pillaging since before recorded history. There will probably be pirates, in one form or another, forever.

Pirate Ships and Their Prey

Through the ages there have been many types of pirating ships. Speed and maneuverability were important, along with cargo space for stolen treasures.

Phoenicians in the eighth century BCE were masters of the Mediterranean, partly due to their boatbuilding skills. Phoenician ships had two tiers, or layers, of oars, and some later vessels even had three banks of oars.

Phoenician ship

From the eighth to eleventh centuries, Vikings explored and plundered from the Baltic seas and European rivers to the British Isles and all the way to Greenland and what is now Canada. Viking long boats were fast, durable, and light. They used rowers, usually slaves, pulling the oars, and had a big square sail.

Viking long boat

The galley, used later, was basically an oared warship, usually with twenty to thirty oars, manned by slaves. They were widely used in the Mediterranean for warfare, but also for trading and sometimes pirating.

Galley ship

Galleons, fully sail-rigged ships, were developed in the fifteenth and sixteenth centuries. Larger and more stable than the galley in rough seas, galleons had more room for artillery and were difficult for invaders to board, faster, and very maneuverable. In addition, galleons held a lot of cargo. The galleon became the backbone of European naval geopolitics across the seas. However, they were heavy and unwieldy. Usually, a galleon holding treasure was the flagship leading a fleet of cargo vessels traveling together for protection against pirate attacks.

Galleon

Pirates liked sailing ships, including sloops, schooners, or smaller brigantines. Sloops have only one mast, and schooners have two or more masts. Brigantines have two masts and some square and some triangular sails. Sailing ships were faster than galleys, had a shallower draft (not as deep in the water as a galleon), and were easier for "hit and run" attacks.

Schooner

Sloop

Small brigantine

Pirate ships in the East were often junks — small family-run boats, and also giant, multi-masted vessels. They had large squarish sails made of bamboo matting with batons (narrow wooden strips) to stiffen the sail.

Junk

Modern pirates use all sorts of vessels. Many are small, private, open boats, with inboard or outboard engines, making them fast, useful to sneak up on a ship, and easy to maneuver.

Open boat

Author's Note

I was raised on the western shore of Maryland's Chesapeake Bay, south of Annapolis. Boating is in my blood. My family always had a boat or two. My dad spent winters building an inboard (occasionally outboard) boat in the garage, using it the next summer for family waterskiing and fishing, selling it in the fall, and then building another one. All four children attended sailing school in the summers. My oldest sibling, Ann, was featured in the local newspaper as the youngest child and first girl around to waterski. She was a winning skipper in the Penguin catboat races in the summer West River Regattas, and later bought a 23-foot sailboat. Brother Rob acquired a classic Chesapeake 20 racing sailboat and restored it. Sister Suzanne is a competitive rower and once worked on an oyster boat, the only one with two women crew members on the Chesapeake Bay. I commuted by outboard to my first job, at a boatyard. After years of powerboats, Dad bought a 40-foot double-headsail wooden yawl designed by Nathaniel Herrschoff, built in 1917. Our family loved the sea, and we vacationed, camping out, on North Carolina's Outer Banks, often going to Ocracoke Island, Blackbeard's hangout.

Years ago, I was a summer sailing counselor at Camp Pinecliffe (Sebago Lake area) in Maine, and I taught sailing for one semester at the University of Maryland. I transferred to the University of Hawaii later to be near the ocean and lived there off and on for five years. I've given art classes and lectured on transatlantic trips on the *QE2* and *Queen Mary II*, taught on Voyages of Discovery and Star Clipper sailing cruises, and traveled by ship in the Mediterranean, Atlantic, Baltic, North Sea, Black Sea, South Pacific, and Caribbean. (In the late 2000s while teaching watercolor art on a sailing cruise in the Caribbean, the ship skipped a port of call due to "suspected pirate activity.") My Scottish great-great-grandfather was a one-armed sea captain (he lost his hand circumnavigating Cape Horn), and my great-grandfather was an engineer on the Cunard (previously White Star) line, traveling all over the world; in those days officers' families came along, and when one of his four children was born, he'd name them after the port they were born in, like Great-Uncle Alexander, born in Egypt.

And now, I get great joy from living on an island called Manhattan and often cross the East River by ferry to my studio in Long Island City.

Index

More About Pirates

Konstam, Angus. *Blackbeard's Last Fight: Pirate Hunting in North Carolina 1718.* Oxford: Osprey Publishing, 2013.

Konstam, Angus. *The Pirate Ship 1660-1730.* Oxford: Osprey Publishing, 2003.

Konstam, Angus and Roger Michael Kean. *Pirates: Predators of the Seas.* New York: Skyhorse Publishing, 2011.

Lehr, Peter. *Pirates: A New History, from Vikings to Somali Raiders.* New Haven and London: Yale University Press, 2019.

Thomas, Graham A. *The Pirate King: The Incredible Story of Captain Henry Morgan.* New York: Skyhorse Publishing, 2015.

Travers, Tim. *Pirates: A History.* Stroud, UK: The History Press, 2009.

Children's Books:

Butterfield, Moira. *Dirty Rotten Pirates: A Truly Revolting Guide to Pirates & Their World.* London: Ticktock, Octopus Publishing Group, 2014.

Menges, Jeff A. *Pirates, Patriots, and Princesses: The Art of Howard Pyle.* Mineola, NY: Dover Publications, Inc., 2006.

Platt, Richard. *Pirate.* New York: DK Publishing, 2004.

Source Notes

p. 6. "She commanded . . . men.": Goldsmith, Maggie. "Ireland's Most Famous Pirate Queen: Grace O'Malley." *Forbes* (November 2022). https://www.forbes.com/sites/margiegoldsmith/2022/11/22/irelands-most-famous-pirate-queen-grace-omalley/

p. 31. "If you had . . . dog.": Kahler, Abbott. "If There's a Man Among Ye: The Tale of Pirate Queens Anne Bonny and Mary Read." *Smithsonian* (August 2011). https://www.smithsonianmag.com/history/if-theres-a-man-among-ye-the-tale-of-pirate-queens-anne-bonny-and-mary-read-45576461/

Sloop

Schooner

Open boat

Small brigantine

Junk